Dorset On A Plate

Hannah Parsons & Gary Kilminster

Foreword by Russell Brown

In aid of Forest Holme Hospice Charity

Registered Charity Number 1038021

Sponsored by Beales Gourmet Ltd

Photography by

www.richardbudd.co.uk

www.partisanphotography.co.uk

This book is dedicated to the patients and staff at Forest Holme Hospice

forest
holme
hospice

FHHC Publishing

Published by FHHC Publishing

Printed by Ashley Press
Unit 2 Brixey Business Park
18-26 Fancy Road
Poole, Dorset

ISBN: 978-0-9926156-0-4

Contents

5   Foreword

8   Forest Holme Hospice

12   Russell Brown

18   Matt Budden

22   Richard Allsopp

26   Beales Gourmet Ltd

32   Maciek Kijewski

38   Samways

40   Luke Stuart

44   Ian Gibbs

48   Simon Hallam

52   Colin Nash

60   Dorset Charcuterie

62   Jack Ingram

68   Andrew Gault

72   Alan Williams

76   Beales Gourmet Ltd

78   Bournemouth & Poole College

80   Dusan Osadsky

84   Adam Baumer

87   Terry Tomlinson

90   Thomas Wickens

93   John Bowler

98   The Escoffier Restaurant

100   Blackacre Farm

102   Gary Kilminster

106   Alistair Willies

110   Ryan Hopper

112   Chris Weight

116   Loic Gratadoux

122   Essential Cuisine

126   Lesley Waters

130   Ashley Palmer-Watts

137   Lyme Bay Winery

138   Dorset on a Plate

140   Ashley Press

141   Richard Budd

142   Index

RB

Foreword By Russell Brown

In the fifteen years that I've been cooking in Dorset there have been many changes, not only in my own life, but in people's interest in cooking, fresh produce and eating out.

Growing up on a farm in Cornwall, fresh produce has been a feature of my life from an early age. Whether it was picking (and quite probably eating!) luscious ripe strawberries fresh from the field, the seductive smell of cakes destined for the farm shop filling the kitchen, or the seemingly endless number of turkeys ready for the Christmas table, I had a real sense of the seasonality of food, even if I didn't recognise it as such at the time.

Years later, opening my own restaurant, Sienna, with my wife Eléna in April 2003, these early influences had an impact on my cooking and I'm sure helped us to gain the Michelin star in 2010.

I still get excited by the first English asparagus, the intoxicating smell of vine tomatoes, gorgeous ripe Scottish raspberries and all the superb meat, fish and game that this area has to offer. Wonderful seasonal produce is one of the biggest triggers for creating new dishes for the restaurant menu.

Coming into the industry at the ripe old age of 27, I started out at the very bottom without any formal training, but there is no doubting the vital role played by college departments such as the Bournemouth School of Hospitality and Food. I have worked with their students on a number of occasions and been struck by both the quality of the students and the commitment of the staff. Catering at a high level requires dedication, passion, ability and an enquiring mind, as the best chefs are often those who avidly read industry articles and cookbooks, eat out whenever they can, and spend some of their days off gaining work experience in other kitchens. All this adds up to a rich pot of knowledge to be drawn on later, and a sound catering college education provides the solid foundation on which to build a fulfilling career.

Specifically in Dorset I feel that the world of food has undergone radical change. The county has always been blessed with some excellent restaurants and superb produce but you only need to take a look in the guide books, on the internet or at social media to see how much this situation has improved.

Restaurants continue to spring up, flourishing artisan producers supply everything from shellfish to cheese to rose veal and the industry continues to increase its appeal as a career.

No journey through life is without its problems and heartache though, so when I was approached by Gary Kilminster, Catering Apprenticeships Co-ordinator at Bournemouth School of Hospitality & Food to write the foreword for this book, I was flattered and more than happy to do so. Forest Holme hospice provides vital support for people with cancer and other life-limiting illnesses; buying this book will help raise much-needed funds to allow them to continue that important role.

I hope you enjoy trying these recipes, donated by some amazing Dorset chefs and the Bournemouth College students; I urge you to cook for your family and friends, eat out at some of the county's wonderful restaurants and derive as much pleasure from food in all its guises as I do.

Russell Brown
Chef Proprietor Sienna Restaurant

HAPPY cooking!

forest holme hospice

Registered Charity No: 1038021

Hidden away in the centre of Poole, Forest Holme hospice is a centre of excellence in the care of those with cancer and other life limiting illnesses. Forest Holme is part of the oncology department of Poole Hospital NHS Foundation Trust and provides specialist end-of-life care to patients in Poole, Wimborne and The Purbecks.

Our teams provide care in the home, inpatient care at the hospice, support for patients within Poole Hospital together with a full range of therapies and treatments. The care extends beyond physical treatment of symptoms; we consider the emotional, psychological, spiritual and social needs of our patients, their families, children and carers.

Forest Holme hospice charity was formed in 1994 to raise funds to support Forest Holme hospice and is now a co-commissioner of many of the services provided at Forest Holme.

Within the hospice, the charity funds two beds in the inpatient ward and additional nursing support. Also housed in the hospice and supported by the charity is the valuable counselling service which supports patients, families and friends who are all affected by life-limiting illnesses. The Hospice-at-Home service is also financially supported by the charity as well as yoga and complementary therapies provided through the Dorset Cancer Centre. Finally, the charity funds the extra special items, which can make life a little bit easier for patients and relatives whilst staying in Forest Holme.

Contact Us

Forest Holme Hospice Charity - 5 Seldown Road, Poole, Dorset BH15 1TS

T: 01202 670644   **E:** fundraising@forestholmehospice.org.uk

Introducing

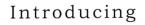

Chef Russell Brown

Chef Matt Budden

Chef Richard Allsopp

Chef Maciek Kijewski

11

Russell Brown - Owner, Sienna Restaurant

Russell Brown found his vocation at the ripe old age of 27. His first full-time cooking job was as a commis chef at the Alverton Manor Hotel in Truro. There he worked under Head Chef Colin Gilbert and was soon chef de partie on the sauce section.

Russell believes that this is a great industry but you do need real passion to succeed and that enjoying the actual craft of what you do is vital. Russell tries to teach chefs how every little job has an effect on the final plate of food, whether that's picking the spinach or scrubbing mussels. Russell's cooking utilises the best seasonal produce to deliver concise menus that show great attention to detail, from the canapés and breads right through to the petit fours.

Russell's first head chef role was at the Yalbury Cottage Hotel just outside Dorchester, where he was awarded 2 AA Rosettes. A move to the Horn of Plenty in Devon followed where Russell worked for Michelin star chef, Peter Gorton.

In 2003 Russell opened Sienna in Dorchester with his wife Eléna. Sienna was awarded a Michelin star in 2010 and has held 3 AA Rosettes since 2007. The restaurant has recently celebrated its 10th anniversary.

Sienna

Sienna is a small restaurant on Dorchester High Street serving a seasonally led menu with the focus on top quality produce, much of it sourced within the West Country. At lunch they serve a two or three course menu, and at dinner they also offer a seven course tasting menu. Sienna has 3 rosettes from the AA and is currently the only Michelin star restaurant in Dorset.

OPENING HOURS
Dinner Tue to Sat 7-9 pm
Lunch Wed to Sat 12.30-2 pm
Reservations required

Sienna Restaurant
36 High West Street
Dorchester, Dorset
DT1 1 UP
T: 01305 250022
browns@siennarestaurant.co.uk
www.siennarestaurant.co.uk

For up to date menus and pricing please visit their web site.
For more information about Russell and to see his blog please visit www.chefrussellbrown.co.uk or follow @siennadorset on Twitter.

Chargrilled veal rump with white bean casserole and pickled carrots

Serves 4

Ingredients

20g butter for cooking veal

4 x 120g portions of English rose veal, from a rump that has been seam-butchered and cut into chunks.

Casserole

1 shallot sliced

1 clove garlic sliced

75ml white wine

200ml fresh vegetable stock

250g cooked white beans (beans sold in jars are ideal)

50ml light olive oil, preferably Arbequina

1tbs chopped flat parsley

Freshly ground black pepper

Pickled carrots

2 large carrots cut into a fine julienne (approximately 8cm long)

Juice of ½ orange

40g cava vinegar or white wine vinegar

40g fresh vegetable stock

1g Maldon sea salt

2g mustard seeds

10g caster sugar

20g light olive oil, preferably Arbequina

Sauce

200g veal trimmings

100ml red wine

2 sprigs of thyme

Olive oil

Method

- **To create the sauce:** In a heavy based pan with a drop of olive oil, colour the veal trimmings, taking them as dark as possible without burning. Keep scraping up the caramelised bits from the bottom of the pan to prevent burning.

- Deglaze with the red wine, again scraping the bottom of the pan well. Allow the wine to reduce to a syrup and then add the thyme. Cover with water and bring to a simmer. Skim well and cook for one hour.

- Pass through a fine sieve into a clean pan, pressing well on the solids. Reduce to around 100ml of liquid. Season to taste and if necessary thicken lightly with corn flour.

- **To create the casserole:** Sweat the shallot and garlic in olive oil until softened but not coloured. A pinch of salt will help. Add the wine and reduce to a syrup, add the vegetable stock and reduce by a third. Add the cooked beans and warm through. Season with Maldon salt and fresh ground black pepper.

- **To create the pickled carrots:** Toast the mustard seeds in a dry pan until they start to pop, then add the orange juice, stock and vinegar. Bring to a simmer and add the salt and sugar. Add the carrot julienne and bring to the boil. Immediately remove from the heat. Stir in the olive oil and allow to cool.

"The sauce, casserole and carrots can all be made in advance and stored in the fridge for up to three days" **Russell Brown** 16

- **To cook the veal**: Season well with Maldon salt and fresh black pepper. Sear on a chargrill plate on all sides.
Transfer to a roasting tin, add 20g melted butter and finish in a hot oven, at 200°C for approximately 4 minutes. You are aiming for medium rare. Allow the veal to rest for around 5 minutes in a warm place.

- **To assemble:** Gently reheat the casserole, add 1tbs chopped flat leaf parsley and divide between 4 bowls. Carve the veal into thick slices and lay onto the beans. Drain and dress the carrots with a little oil and Maldon salt. Pile the carrots onto the veal. Reheat the sauce and pour over and around the veal.
Finish with a drizzle of Arbequina olive oil.

Photo by Richard Budd

Matt Budden - Executive Head Chef, Highcliff Grill

Matt Budden is the Executive Head Chef at the 4 star Bournemouth Highcliff Marriott Hotel and the 2AA Rosette Highcliff Grill.

Matt is also responsible for the hotel's extensive food offering and can often be seen giving demonstrations at local food festivals and writing for his food blog. Matt is a real foodie whether it is ingredients, dishes, stories or just random food knowledge.

Matt brings with him years of experience as an Executive Chef. He has extensive experience around the world in Australia, New Zealand and Vietnam and has headed up many prestigious kitchen brigades, most recently at the Grand Harbour Hotel, Rhinefield House Hotel and at the Goodwood Estate for Lord March.

Matt brings with him a passion for culinary excellence and a keen eye on developing talent, dedicated to ensuring that young talented chefs get the best start in the industry. Matt is a proud member of the prestigious *Master Chefs of Great Britain* since 2004 and has been awarded runner up in the 'Independent on Saturday' Chef of the Year food awards.

The Bournemouth Highcliff Marriott Hotel
St Michaels Road - West Cliff - Bournemouth - Dorset - BH2 5DU

This iconic hotel in Dorset, built in 1873, has a cliff top location boasting panoramic views of the sea and seven miles of golden beaches. Adjacent to Bournemouth International Centre, this 4-star hotel is an ideal location to explore local attractions on the Dorset coast. Guests can enjoy culinary surprises from Executive Chef Matt Budden with innovative cuisine from their Taste of Dorset menu in the award-winning 2 AA Rosette Highcliff Grill.

The Highcliff Grill believes in serving the best locally sourced fish, shellfish and fine wines in a relaxed stunning location. They believe in adapting classic dishes the modern palate, producing dishes that are simple but elegant, introducing some unexpected but carefully considered flavour combinations to thrill the taste buds.
The Highcliff Grill menus are inspired by the 'Farm to Fork' Philosophy and the 'Future Fish' concept which gives their guests the best sustainable produce. They source local Dorset and Hampshire produce buying from local farmers and fishermen, that they have visited to ensure quality and sustainability in all of their produce so that they can showcase the very best and sometimes forgotten food that can be produced in this country.

T: 01202 557702
www.highcliffgrill.co.uk

Dorset brown crab with cucumber, radish and crisp pea shoots
Serves 4

Ingredients

50ml mayonnaise

125g cornflour

1 whole cucumber

1 tbsp cider vinegar

Handful of pea shoots

Selection of micro herbs

100ml sparkling water

Sea salt and black pepper

1 whole Dorset brown crab

2 leaves of softened gelatine

1 breakfast radish, sliced thinly

1 tbsp finely chopped flat leaf parsley

1 tbsp finely chopped spring onion and chives

Method

♦   Bring to the boil a large heavy based pan of heavily salted water. Blanch the whole crab for 4 minutes per 500g of crab.

♦   Remove from water carefully and let the crab cool naturally, once cool remove the legs and put to one side. Turn crab over with underbelly facing away from you, and use both of your thumbs to push out the underbelly to reveal the brown meat. Crack open the legs with the reverse of a heavy cook's knife, remove white meat and pick through, carefully removing any shell.

♦   Remove all of the brown meat from the main shell. It is vital you remove the grey gills from the body, called 'dead man's fingers' as these are very tough and indigestible.

20

- Mix the white meat with a little mayonnaise and the spring onion and chive mix, adding just enough mayonnaise to bind together. Mix the brown meat with the chopped flat leaf parsley and season to taste.

- Chop the cucumber into rough dice and puree in a blender. Pass through a sieve and reserve the cucumber juice.

- Warm the vinegar through in a heavy based saucepan and add the softened gelatine so that it dissolves. Mix this liquor with the cucumber juice and then pour into serving bowls and leave to set in the fridge for a minimum of two hours.

- Make the tempura batter for the pea shoots by whisking the cornflour with the sparkling water (you may not need all of the water so add a little at a time).

- To finish the dish place the brown meat into an individual metal ring on top of the jelly and top with the white meat. Carefully remove the ring.

- Coat the pea shoots with the batter and shallow fry until crisp and golden.

- Remove and place on kitchen towel to remove any excess oil.

- Top the crab with the micro herbs and radishes and scatter over the crisp pea shoots.

Richard Allsopp - Executive Chef, Menzies Hotels

Richard Allsopp first developed his passion for cooking during food technology classes at school. On Saturdays, Richard would visit Birmingham market and was amazed by the variety of seafood on display. Richard and his father would walk around the market eating whelks and winkles and would often take home fresh herring roes for Saturday lunch. After finishing college, Richard began working at The Belfry Hotel in Sutton Coldfield. Richard received great encouragement from the executive chef at The Belfry, Mr Eric Bruce, who introduced him to culinary competitions throughout Britain, Ireland and Canada. Richard now works as Executive Chef at the Menzies Hotels in Bournemouth. His love of seafood has inspired his menu and he is proud to use local fish supplier, Hutching Brothers, who source fish from Mudeford Quay in Dorset.

The Menzies Bournemouth Carlton and East Cliff Court Hotels

Having recently undergone refurbishments, The Menzies Bournemouth Carlton and East Cliff Court Hotels are two of the most iconic hotels on the South Coast. The hotels differ in decor with the East Cliff Court offering a more contemporary feel with its bright, modern interior and the Carlton Hotel having grand charm and richly decorated reception areas and lounges. You can relax in style and comfort at both hotels, and savour a splendid meal in the superb restaurants against the sparkling backdrop of the sea.

For an impressive hotel with spectacular sea views, 4-star facilities and service, The Menzies Hotels are the perfect choice.

Steamed Christchurch Bay turbot fillet, roasted scallop, lobster mash with lobster sauce

Serves 4

Ingredients

4 x 110g fillets of turbot

4 x large scallops

1 x small lobster (cooked and shelled)

200g potato puree

½ a tsp English mustard

10g finely chopped chives

25g chopped shallots

½ clove crushed garlic

Olive oil

25g butter

½ lemon

500ml fish stock

Crushed lobster shells

25g tomato puree paste

50ml Pernod

100g mirepoix (*roughly diced carrot, onion & celery*)

1 star anise

1 bay leaf

Method

- **Making the sauce:** In a saucepan heat a little olive oil and lightly sweat off the mirepoix until soft but adding no colour. Add the tomato puree paste, fish stock, star anise and bay leaf, and reduce by half. Add the white wine and Pernod, reduce by one third, pass through a fine strainer and whisk in unsalted butter. Correct seasoning and keep warm.

- **Making the lobster mash:** Leaving the two lobster claw meat to one side, chop the remaining tail and leg meat. In a saucepan heat a little olive oil and sweat off the chopped shallots and garlic. Add chopped lobster meat, mustard and chopped chives. Add potato puree, gently heat through, add butter, correct seasoning and place in a piping bag and keep warm.

- **Cooking the seafood:** In a small steamer add the four pieces of turbot and two lobster claws. Season with salt, lemon juice and white pepper. Heat a non stick frying pan with a little olive oil, when hot added scallops and quickly reduce heat to half. Add a knob of butter and after 30 seconds the scallops should be caramelized on one side. Turn scallops over and cook for a further 30 seconds. Remove all seafood from cooking process and keep warm.

- **To plate:** Pipe the lobster mash in the centre of four bowls. Arrange the turbot fillets on top with a scallop on each fillet and half a lobster claw. Surround the lobster mash with sauce and serve.

Introduction to Beales Gourmet

After his return from the gastronomic haven of France in 2005, Chef and Managing Director Tony Beales dreamed about having a company that would create innovative and bespoke menus – a company that would never compromise on food quality and a company that put that the desires of customers first. Soon his ambition, to create an elite local catering company that would bring delight to diners at any occasion, started to unfold and Beales Gourmet Ltd was born. Having worked as a chef in a wide variety of exclusive establishments, Tony knew just what he was looking for in building the perfect team to make Beales Gourmet the most desirable caterers on the South Coast. The team now consists of the very best local chefs, precise service staff and a knowledgeable sales team all sharing his vision and enthusiasm to create the most sensational cuisine, delivered with absolute precision.

Tony Beales

Beales Gourmet services

As one of the region's leading catering
companies, Beales Gourmet services include:

- Bespoke wedding reception catering
- Gourmet barbecues & spit roasts
- Canapé and drinks receptions
- High profile corporate events
- Themed celebration parties
- Exquisite marquee catering
- Glamorous garden parties
- Intimate home dining

The friendly and professional team at Beales Gourmet
are always delighted to help you plan the perfect event,
whatever the occasion. Receive a tailor-made menu package
quotation with no obligation, or visit their website to view
sample menus and prices. The Beales Gourmet office
is open Monday to Saturday from 9am to 6pm.

T: 01202 700992
info@bealesgourmet.com
www.bealesgourmet.com

EXCLUSIVE
BEALES
GOURMET
CATERING

What can Beales Gourmet do for you?

Weddings

Great food and outstanding service are essential elements to enhance the success of any wedding. After years of experience within the wedding industry, Beales Gourmet can offer an exclusive wedding catering service that your guests will remember forever.

Let their enthusiastic team share their experience with you and offer advice about all aspects of your wedding arrangements.

Your wedding menus can be tailored to suit your individual culinary requirements and most importantly your personal catering budget.

No matter which venue you choose for your dream wedding, Beales Gourmet will maintain the consistent high level of service that customers have come to expect.

Private Dining

Hosting the perfect dinner party or cocktail reception couldn't be easier or more stress free. Let Beales Gourmet take away all the stress of catering your own party at home. They can take care of every aspect of the party, from cooking through to clearing up, you needn't worry about a thing!

Corporate Dining

One area where Beales Gourmet has excelled is in the delivery of high-end catering for countless corporate events. From awards dinners to product launches, director's lunches or networking events, the team at Beales Gourmet has the experience, passion and creativity to lift your corporate event to gastronomic heights.

The Italian Villa

Wherever you choose to host your event, Beales Gourmet will ensure it is a spectacular occasion for you. Home to their kitchen and head office, the wonderful Italian Villa is set within the 10 acres of beautiful historic gardens of Compton Acres, near the exclusive area of Sandbanks. Walking distance to luxury hotels and beaches, and with ample car parking, this venue has the grandeur to deliver unforgettable events.

As the only one of its kind in the UK, The Italian Villa offers three stunning floors of unrivalled elegance to lay on the perfect event. Over three floors, the grand Villa gives a feel different to any other venue, leaving hosts never having to worry about "other guests at a hotel", or "staff attending to other matters". At The Italian Villa, their guests are their ONLY priority! Impeccable standards ensure that every guest feels like a VIP.

Combined with direct access into the spectacular Italian Garden, The Villa can cater for small, intimate events from 50 guests, or can provide a relaxed setting for up to 250 guests when using the Italian Garden. Well appointed with lifts to all three floors, air conditioning, built in sound systems and speakers, a stage, and audiovisual screens, The Villa's superb facilities help to create a truly memorable occasion every time.

Further afield

If you prefer another fabulous, historic or unique location, Beales Gourmet are nominated caterers for the following exclusive venues:

- Highcliffe Castle
- Lulworth Castle
- Winchester Guildhall
- Harry Warren House
- The Victorian Barn

- The Orangery Suit
- The Lighthouse
- Sopley Mill
- Upton Country Park
- Marquee events

Maciek Kijewski – Beales Gourmet

Head Chef for favourite local caterers, Beales Gourmet, Maciek Kijewski (nicknamed Magic by colleagues), creates that exact magic by fusing traditional English food with a touch of Italian and modern, molecular cookery – creating unusual textures and tastes such as foams, fizzes and jellies.

He says: *"As well as creating lovely flavours, I'm an artist – every plate we serve should be a work of art. I love food, I love experimenting with new ideas and am creating new dishes in my head all the time - it's not unusual for me to dream up recipes in my sleep."*

Maciek, who moved to the UK from Poland in 2004, has a wealth of experience: as well as having worked as senior sous chef at the Marriott Hotel, he's cooked aboard HMS Ark Royal and catered a series of large events at the Top Gear Racing Circuit, the Henley Royal Regatta and Eastbourne Tennis. Maciek will continue to lead the busy team at Beales Gourmet, creating bespoke menus both for events at the Italian Villa and providing catering for events at popular venues throughout the region.

Father of one, Maciek, has already
developed a Beales Gourmet signature
dish - Duet of lamb (tenderloin and cutlet)
with a beetroot and black onion seed
mash, star anise-infused squash puree
and minted pea and broad bean dressing.

EXCLUSIVE
BEALES
GOURMET
CATERING

Duet of spring Dorset lamb

Serves 4

Ingredients

500g lamb shoulder (boned)

2 litres goose fat

6 cloves of garlic

Half a bunch of rosemary, thyme, bayleaf and sage

4 French trimmed lamb cutlets (90g each)

100ml herb and garlic oil

500g Maris piper potatoes

100ml olive oil

2 star anise

500ml fresh beetroot juice

1 tsp black onion seeds

1 butternut squash, diced

125g butter

1 cube of brown sugar

20g fresh peas

20g fresh peeled broad beans

½ bunch fresh mint

1 bunch fresh pea shoots

150ml red wine jus

Method

♦ Cover the lamb shoulder with melted goose fat and cook (confit) at 80°C for 8 hours or until tender. Add garlic and fresh mixed herbs to the goose fat to taste. When cooked, flake the meat and roll into a ballotine or press between two trays. Leave to set in the fridge.

♦ Marinate the lamb cutlets in herb and garlic oil overnight. Seal the lamb 'pink' just before serving but allow to rest for at least 5 minutes before serving.

♦ Boil the potatoes and cook until tender. Make a smooth mash by combining the potatoes with 100ml of olive oil.

♦ Create a beetroot puree by reducing the fresh beetroot juice until a syrup consistency is formed. Add the beetroot puree and black onion seeds to the mash potato. Keep warm.

♦ To make a butternut squash puree, add the diced butternut squash to a pan and half cover with water. Add the butter, star anise and brown sugar and bring to the boil. Once tender, remove the star anise, drain well, and blend. Continue to blend the mixture until a smooth puree has formed.

♦ Cook the peas and broad beans till 'al dente' and mix with olive oil and fresh torn mint and serve warm. Cut the chilled confit shoulder in to four squares or cylinders and pan fry just before serving to add colour and heat through.

♦ Serve all together with the red wine jus and garnish with fresh pea shoots.

Jurassic Coast scallops, trio of cauliflower, crispy pancetta, with a baby caper dressing
Serves 4

Ingredients

12 fresh scallops

150g purple cauliflower

100g romanesco cauliflower, cut into 1cm pieces

100g white cauliflower, cut into 1cm pieces

50g butter

30ml olive oil

10ml chardonnay vinegar

Sprinkle of garlic chives

Seasoning

For the dressing

10ml truffle oil

5g crushed garlic

10g fresh thyme

200g pancetta in cubes

25g baby capers

30g chopped parsley

Method

- Wipe the scallops with a dry cloth and remove the muscle and coral.

- Cook the cauliflowers in boiling water till 'al dente'. Add the chardonnay vinegar to the small pieces of white cauliflower and romanesco cauliflower and set aside to garnish the dish.

- Make a smooth puree from the purple cauliflower with the butter and olive oil, season to taste.

- For the dressing, slowly fry the pancetta until all the fat has separated and the pancetta is golden brown and crispy.

- Remove the pancetta from the heat. Add the garlic, truffle oil, fresh thyme, parsley and baby capers to the pan, mix together.

- To serve, sear the scallops in a very hot pan with olive oil until caramelized and golden brown, approximately 1 minute on each side. Make a swoosh with the purple cauliflower puree, add the scallops, drizzle the dressing over the scallops and garnish with the pieces of cauliflower and garlic chives.

Maciek's Tip
This photograph shows an additional garnish of citrus foam. This is a secret recipe created by Beales Gourmet Ltd

SAMWAYS
Fish Merchants & International Transporters

Samways Fish Merchants is and has always been a family run business, established in 1961 by Mr Clifford Samways from a small wooden barrow, selling his catch on the harbour of West Bay, Dorset.

Fifty years on, Samways Fish Merchants has grown into a thriving local business with a purpose built factory, a great product range and a good team providing an extremely efficient service, led by Clive Samways, Managing Director since 1985. Clive headed a huge push into the European market which now boasts a very strong export team, which also led Samways to become international transporters, with their own refrigerated trucks and drivers.

Clive's wife, Sarah, joined the team in the 1999 to drive forward the catering side of the business which now has a client list of hundreds of customers. Their purpose built factory at Gore Cross, Bridport now has 70 employees to handle all of their customers' requests. Samways are in direct communication with over 150 inshore boats on a daily basis. The relationship with the skippers of each individual vessel is paramount to Samways, ensuring that the South Coast fish that they catch is looked after to the highest possible standards.

Samways currently supplies over 600 tonnes of fish back to fishermen for shellfish capture, who can then land their catch back to them for their various customers. Samways believe that 'local' is the key and their motto is *port to plate in 24 hours!*

T: 01308 424496

www.samwaysfish.com

Introducing

Chef Luke Stuart

Chef Ian Gibbs

Chef Simon Hallam

Chef Colin Nash

Luke Stuart - Curator, White Pepper Cookery

Luke Stuart is the curator of White Pepper, a multi award winning cookery school located in the picturesque and rural setting of Bere Farm, East Dorset - just a stone's throw away from Poole Harbour, Sandbanks and the Jurassic Coast.

Luke, who recently won the Blackmore Vale Business Award for Young Entrepreneur of the Year, is an experienced chef and a qualified teacher. Luke has worked in London and throughout the Mediterranean and Caribbean and also for the Rouxs, Tom Conran and Ivana Trump. He was a senior chef tutor for Tante Marie Culinary Academy, part owned by Gordon Ramsay.

WHITE PEPPER
COOKERY SCHOOL

White Pepper arguably has one of the most comprehensive portfolios of cookery courses and food experiences in the UK. The Cookery School offers more than 30 courses aimed at enthusiastic cooks/chefs (from beginner to professional), bespoke cookery days, corporate cookery packages and a cookery school for children. Driven by a passion for quality food and first class teaching, White Pepper courses teach the *how* and *why* of cookery in a relaxed and engaging way.

White Pepper was nominated 'finalist' in the category Best Short Cookery Course by The UK Cookery School Awards 2012.

The School has a very strong affiliation with schools, youth groups, charities and local producers receiving the following nominations in 2012: Best Community Engagement (Finalist) British Cookery School Awards, Best Community Focused School (Finalist) UK Cookery School Awards.

The friendly team at White Pepper is made up of professional chefs, qualified teachers and Dorset food producers and would encourage you to visit the website and also drop into the school at Bere Farm.

Bere Farm Cottages, Wareham Rd, Lytchett Minster, Dorset, BH16 6F

Warm chocolate fondant
Serves 4

Ingredients

Chocolate centre

75g dark chocolate, chopped

5 tbsp double cream

Sponge

30g unsalted butter

150g dark chocolate, chopped

2 eggs, separated

1½ egg whites (3 ½ whites in total)

45g caster sugar

NB: You will need four ovenproof and non-stick pudding basins or Dariole moulds.

Grease the moulds with butter and flour (or butter and cocoa).

42

Method
Pre-heat the oven to 180°C

♦ **Making the chocolate centre**: Heat the cream until it begins to boil. Pour on to the chopped chocolate and stir until fully incorporated. Place in the fridge and allow to set, approximately 45-60 minutes.

♦ **Making the sponge**: Gently melt the butter and chocolate in a saucepan. Remove from the heat and put to one side.

♦ Place the 3½ egg whites into a clean bowl and whisk until stiff. Add the sugar 1 tbsp at a time, continuing to whisk all the time, the whites should appear stiff and glossy.

♦ Enrich the chocolate mixture with the egg yolks and mix until fully incorporated. Then fold the egg whites into the chocolate mixture in three batches.

♦ Remove the chocolate centre from the fridge and roll into four walnut sized balls. Fill the moulds with half the sponge mixture. Place a chocolate ball on top. Place the remaining mixture on top and level the top of the moulds.

♦ Bake for approximately 12 minutes or until springy and well risen. The edge of the sponge should also leave the sides of the mould.

♦ The sponge mixture will keep for an hour if it is covered with cling film. Overcooking will result in a solid sponge with no liquid centre. Check after 10 minutes. Serve hot with ice cream rolled in chopped nuts. **43**

Ian Gibbs - Kings Arms

After training in the Midlands under professional competition
organiser Peter Griffiths M.B.E, Ian became very successful in the
competition circuit winning many live medals in London and across
the country including Rioja Chef of the Year and more recently
Dorset and Hampshire Chef of the Year.

In 2003 Ian was selected to cook for HRH The Queen and HRH The Duke
of Edinburgh at Gloucester Cathedral for the Maundy Thursday Service.
After working in the Cotswolds, which gave him a great passion for
using local produce, he moved to Dorset and achieved many awards
at the Coventry Arms, Corfe Mullen. After working in and around
Bournemouth, Ian is now working for local renowned chef,
Alex Aitken, at the Kings Arms in Christchurch allowing him to
further his knowledge of local Dorset and New Forest produce.

The Kings Arms

The Kings Arms in Christchurch is a stunning Georgian building in the heart of Dorset, combining a traditional yet stylish restaurant with luxurious bedrooms carefully restored in true Georgian style. Whilst Alex Aitken remains chef patron at The Jetty he is also spending time with the chefs at The Kings Arms headed by Ian Gibbs. The restaurant serves the very best local and seasonal food with sophisticated simplicity and a unique and charming English setting, overlooking the Kings Arms Bowling Green and historical castle ruins. The Kings Restaurant is honoured to introduce the new 'Josper Grill', a technique that imparts a distinctive charcoal flavour to all the local and handpicked ingredients placed upon its coals. The delicious menu makes use of the very best local ingredients either caught, grown or prepared close to Christchurch from the New Forest and the waters of the South Coast.

T: 01202 588933
www.thekings-christchurch.co.uk

Slow roast hand of Meadowbrook Farm pork, pearl barley, smoked bacon and thyme cassoulet

Serves 2

Ingredients

1 pork hand, boned and tied

1 litre chicken stock

250g soaked pearl barley

50g smoked streaky bacon

4 sprigs of thyme

50g shredded baby spinach

1 litre vegetable stock

25ml double cream

1 onion, diced

1 clove garlic, crushed

50ml jus/gravy

Pea shoots for garnish

Butter for cooking

Method

♦ Place the pork hand in chicken stock in a deep oven tray, cover the top with foil and slow braise in the oven at 150°C for 2-3 hours.

♦ Remove from the stock to cool, then divide the pork hand into two equal portions.

♦ Boil the pearl barley in the vegetable stock until tender, drain and reserve.

♦ Sauté onion, garlic and thyme in butter, add barley and double cream, add the smoked bacon and finish with the baby spinach.

♦ To plate, place the pearl barley risotto in the centre of a plate or large bowl. Place some pea shoots on top, place the hand of pork on top of pea shoots, drizzle jus over the pork.

Simon Hallam - Crooked Beam Restaurant

Like many of the great culinary masters of past and present,
Simon Hallam started his career at a tender age, observing his
grandmother as she cooked. This home grown inspiration saw
cooking become his passion. After completing his training in
Northampton, Simon moved south to progress his career.
Classing himself as an 'all-rounder', Simon's style is traditional with
a modern twist. Simon has been the chef proprietor of the AA Rosette
awarded Crooked Beam Restaurant for over 8 years and continues to
develop his award winning style of cooking and presentation to
ensure that every dish leaving his kitchen offers perfect,
mouth-watering food, presented with unique style and optimum
quality and taste.

The Crooked Beam is a family owned, family run restaurant of the highest order. Proprietors Simon and Vicki Hallam head a group of friendly staff, dedicated to providing the very best food and service, with original menus featuring traditional food with a modern twist.

The restaurant blends a traditional 'Olde Worlde' past with modern comfort and cultured ambience to create a unique style, quite unlike any other.

In any fine restaurant the most important aspect is the food. At the Crooked Beam, Simon runs a busy kitchen to the highest standards of hygiene, preparation, cooking and presentation, ensuring that every dish that leaves his kitchen is prepared to order from fresh ingredients and to the highest quality.

Awarded its sixth consecutive AA Rosette, the Crooked Beam kitchen continues to raise the standards of fine dining in the Dorset area. The Crooked Beam prides itself on producing the highest quality traditional food and signature dishes to exacting standards, presented with panache and served with a smile.

2 The Grove, Christchurch, Dorset, BH23 2HA.
T: 01202 499362 **49**

Lamb two ways served with Boulangere potatoes

Serves 4

Ingredients

250g mirepoix (diced carrot, onion and celery)

1 bulb garlic, broken into cloves

1 litre veal stock

1 large bunch fresh rosemary

2 kg lamb shoulder (with bone)

Freshly ground black pepper

5ml mint sauce

10g redcurrant jelly

4 x lamb rumps

30ml rapeseed oil

Boulangere potatoes

1kg potatoes (Maris piper)

1 large onion

600ml stock

Olive oil

Salt and pepper

Method

- Heat a pan, add the oil and seal the lamb shoulder. Once sealed, season and remove from pan. Add the diced vegetables and garlic to the pan, sauté until coloured, place in roasting tray and sit the lamb shoulder on top. Add rosemary and stock and cover with foil. Slowly cook for 2 hours at 150°C.

- Slice the potatoes and onions and layer in a oven proof dish, seasoning each layer. Add the stock and cook in the oven for 35-45 minutes at 150°C until tender.

- Remove lamb shoulder and leave to cool until able to handle, pull the meat from the bone and shred.

- Strain liquid from roasting tin and reduce by three quarters. Add redcurrant jelly and mint sauce and reduce until it coats the back of a spoon.

- Heat a frying pan and add oil. Brown all sides of lamb rump, season and finish in oven for 6-8 minutes at 170°C. Remove from the oven and leave to rest.

- Mix a little sauce with the shredded lamb press into a metal ring and reheat in the oven. Remove from the oven and place on serving plate. Carefully remove the ring, slice the rump and place on plate. Drizzle the dish with the sauce reduction and serve with boulangere potatoes.

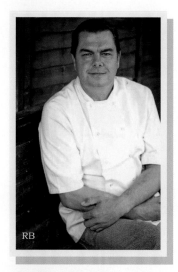

RB

Colin Nash - The Three Tuns

Colin Nash is renowned for his relentless pursuit of innovation in his kitchen. With over 30 years of experience, Colin is one of the most exciting chefs in Dorset, winning many awards for The Three Tuns over his 5 years in the kitchen.

His career began at the young age of 13 helping his mum in local restaurants in Christchurch. After school he wasted no time in enrolling in Bournemouth and Poole catering college, one of the best colleges in England. This led him to Langans Brasserie in the heart of London, his first taste of pressure in a busy kitchen. As years went by he developed a passion and understanding of what he wanted to achieve by working in various hotels and restaurants along the way.

In 2007 Colin left Stanwell House Hotel in Lymington to join The Three Tuns, making an immediate impact by winning 2 Rosettes for the pub in his second year. He prides himself on fresh local and seasonal foods and likes to add the occasional twist. *"A good meal is like a good movie exciting you along the way"* he quotes.

The Three Tuns

Situated on the edge of the New Forest Country Park, and a pleasant three mile drive from Christchurch and Burley

The Three Tuns is an award-winning traditional 17th century inn with huge acclaim for its excellent food and drink. The Three Tuns boasts creative menus, daily specials, five cask marque awarded ales and a very warm welcome from its owner and the "Tuns Team". Its popularity continues to grow with both locals and visitors alike.

The 60 seat restaurant offers excellent food using the finest fresh produce, seasonal specials, classic dishes and an exciting fusion of seasonings from around the world. Head chef Colin Nash and his team have been recognised by both local and national food critics and the Egon Ronay Guide for their culinary expertise. The restaurant has also been awarded two AA rosettes for their high quality of food.

Tel: 01425 672232
www.threetunsinn.com

Garlic king prawns and red mullet in miso broth, baby pak choi, broccoli, enoki mushrooms and potatoes

Serves 4

Ingredients

600g red mullet fillets
(*divided into 4 portions*)
12 king prawns
100g miso paste
2 baby pak choi
50g enoki mushrooms
4 cooked new potatoes
1 small onion
1 carrot

1 stick of celery
1 small leek
1 litre of cold water
2 tbsp dark soy sauce
2 cloves of garlic
1 head of broccoli
1 tsp sugar
A little sesame oil
Salt and pepper to taste

Photo by Richard Budd

Method

♦ Wash, peel and chop the onion, carrot, celery and leek and fry in a saucepan in oil until slightly brown. Add one clove of crushed garlic, the miso paste, soy sauce, sugar and water, bring to the boil and simmer for 2 hours. If the liquid reduces below the line of the vegetables add a little more water and keep the vegetables covered in juice. Pass through a fine sieve into a new saucepan and discard the vegetables. Taste the sauce and add a little more water if you find it to be too strong in flavour. Season with a little salt and pepper to get the flavour how you like it being cautious with the salt. Leave to cool on the side.

♦ Wash, trim and cut the pak choi into 8 pieces slicing lengthways and add to the strained miso broth. Wash and cut the broccoli into small florets and add to the broth together with wedges of new potatoes and trimmed enoki mushrooms.

♦ Heat up a heavy frying pan till very hot then add a little oil and the other clove of garlic (slightly crushed), season and fry the red mullet fillets skin side down pressing the fish against the pan to prevent them curling up for 20 seconds. Fry for about 1 minute so the skin goes crispy and a light golden colour. Turn the fillets carefully and then add the prawns to the pan; fry for 1 minute and turn them again carefully. Remove from the heat and leave to rest for a couple of minutes; they will both continue cooking without heat.

♦ Meanwhile bring thr broth back to the boil and simmer for 3-4 minutes with a lid on the saucepan. Assemble into 4 bowls and arrange the fish on top and serve. **55**

Recipe by Colin Nash
Refer to page 54

Photo by Richard Budd

Photo by Alan Williams

Recipe by Richard Allsopp
Refer to page 24

THE DORSET CHARCUTERIE
COMPANY

A real butcher shop knows the true provenance of their meat, they hang it properly, understand the cuts and know how best to cook it. Dorset Charcuterie goes one step further and turns their high provenance meat into artisan handmade Charcuterie.

Purveyors of real handmade cured, smoked and air-dried meats, Lee Moreton and Benjamin Sugden, set Dorset Charcuterie up with the help of The Princes Trust in 2010 and turned a joint passion for salami, pâtés and other air-dried meats into a successful business.

Set on a working beef and arable farm close to the beautiful Purbeck hills, the Butcher Boys source the best local, free range and wild meats from as close to their butchery/charcuterie as possible. Lee and Ben use a mix of traditional methods like dry curing and smoking coupled with more modern techniques like sous vide to create award winning products such as; Dorset Smoked Chaps, Black Pudding, Pâtés, Terrines, Dorset Air-Dried Ham, Collar and Loin and a growing selection of Dorset Salami.

The boys have created a quirky onsite Deli that showcases Dorset as a true foodie county. Dorset Charcuterie believe strongly in teaching others about the importance of knowing where your food comes from and helping others to recognise a passion for finding, making and eating good local food.

For further information regarding Lee and Ben's Deli, Butchery, Charcuterie and courses, please visit their website and sign up to their mailing list.

www.dorsetcharcuterie.co.uk

Introducing

Chef Jack Ingram

Chef Andrew Gault

Chef Alan Williams

Jack Ingram - Bistro Vue, Melbourne

Jack was born in Dorchester and grew up in Maiden Newton.
His first job was at Le Petit Canard. Cooking always fascinated him
and he loved watching the chefs in the kitchen. This led Jack to study
hospitality & catering at college. After a few years of working in
excellent restaurants in the UK, Jack decided it was time to spread
his wings and travelled to Australia. He settled in South Australia
working at the award winning Southern Ocean Lodge. After a year,
he decided it was time to head for the bright lights of Melbourne and
started working at the 3 Hat restaurant, Vue de Monde, under Head
Chef Shannon Bennett. Jack has worked for Shannon for over 3 years
and is currently the Head Chef at the sister restaurant, Bistro Vue.
Jack's inspiration from a young age has been his mother and
grandmother, who are both fantastic cooks and created his love of
food. Jack draws inspiration from all the chefs he has worked with
over the past 10 years.

He says *"The adrenaline and satisfaction I get from producing the
perfect plate of food makes the 17 hour days worthwhile"*. **62**

Ingredients and Method

Pigeon

2 pigeons
2 sprigs of thyme
100g butter
Sea salt
Olive oil for pan frying

Remove the legs, wings and the back-bone from the pigeon (you can ask your butcher to do this), and reserve the bones for the sauce. Season the pigeon with the sea salt and place a sprig of thyme on each pigeon breast. Place the pigeon crowns in individual sous vide bags with 25g of butter and vacuum seal. Cook the pigeon crowns in a water bath at 58°C for 15 minutes. Remove from the water bath and allow to rest for 10 minutes in the bag. Heat a medium sauté pan with a little olive oil on high heat, remove the pigeon crowns from the vacuum bag and pat dry with paper towel. Take the pigeon breast and place it side down and colour until golden, repeat this both sides with all 4 breasts. Add the remaining butter and baste the pigeon for 1 minute. Remove from the pan and rest again for 5 – 7 minutes upside down to allow the juices to rest back through the breast.

Jerusalem artichoke puree

300g Jerusalem artichokes
100ml water
500ml milk
Sea salt

64

Wash and peel the artichokes, cut in half and cook until tender in the water and milk (the water stops the milk from burning). Once tender strain the artichokes and reserve the cooking liquid. Blend the artichokes with one third of the cooking liquid on high speed until you have a smooth, silky puree. Season with sea salt. Place to the side and keep warm.

Autumn vegetable fricassee

6 medium size Jerusalem artichokes

6 baby beetroots

1 medium sized parsnip

12 baby carrots

6 medium sized pine mushrooms

5 brussel sprouts

50g butter

2 litres chicken stock

2 sprigs of thyme

Wash and peel the artichokes and baby carrots. Peel, quarter and core the parsnip. Braise them all in the chicken stock until tender. Remove from the stock, cut the artichokes in half and refresh all with ice water. Place to the side. Boil the baby beetroots in their skin until tender. Strain and peel when they are still warm. Quarter and reserve. Wash the pine mushrooms. Quarter and reserve.
Peel individual leaves off the brussel sprouts. Reserve. Heat a large sauté pan with a little olive oil on high heat. First, add the artichokes and parsnip and get a golden colour on all sides. Then, add the carrots and pine mushrooms and sauté for a further 2 minutes, add the beetroot and butter and roast for another 2 minutes. Deglaze with a little chicken stock and finally add the brussel sprout leaves, remove from the heat so the sprout leaves only just cook and still look alive.

Lentil jus

100g du Puy lentils (cooked in chicken stock until tender)
Pigeon bones, legs and wings
1 litre veal stock
200ml red wine
5 sprigs thyme
10 juniper berries
1 bay leaf
50g butter
2 shallots

Roast the pigeon bones, legs and wings in an oven preheated to 200°C until golden (approximately 40 minutes). Meanwhile in a heavy based saucepan foam the butter and sauté the sliced shallots until translucent, add the roasted bones and the red wine, reduce the wine by two thirds until it starts to get syrupy. Add the veal stock, thyme, bay and juniper leaf. Bring to a simmer on a medium heat and allow to reduce by almost half, skimming frequently. Strain through a fine sieve and discard the bones. Add the lentils to the jus and reserve ready for plating.

To finish

2 Roasted and rested pigeon crowns
Jerusalem artichoke puree
Autumn vegetable fricassee
Lentil jus
Pineapple sage

To assemble the dish spread a large tablespoon of the artichoke puree across the left hand side of the dish, build the vegetable fricassee on top of the puree starting with the artichokes, pine mushrooms and beetroots, place the carrots around in a natural fashion giving the dish height. Finish with the brussel sprout leaves, broad bean flowers and pineapple sage. Carve the breasts off the pigeon and place one on each plate next to the vegetables. Finish with the lentil jus.

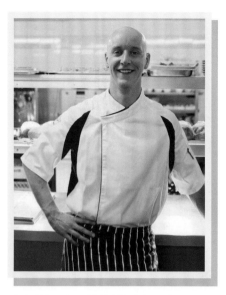

Andrew Gault - Head Chef, Captain's Club Hotel & Spa

Andrew Gault has been Head Chef at the Captain's Club Hotel & Spa since it opened its doors in November 2006. Andrews's career has taken him to several different countries to live and work including Scotland, France, Ireland and Dubai, but he particularly enjoys working with the local produce that the South Coast offer's from the asparagus in the New Forest, seafood from the Solent and the lamb from all across the South Coast. The career highlight for Andrew would have to be the involvement since the beginning of Captains Club Hotel, Andrew says; *'Anybody that has been involved in a hotel from the beginning will understand the work involved both physically and mentally and to see it grow is very rewarding'.*
Having met a number of celebrity chefs throughout his career Andrew says Keith Floyd has been a huge inspiration to him. Keith was a natural chef, cooking food in the 80s that most people had never heard of but he was also very good at making food what it should be .... fun!

Captain's Club Hotel & Spa

The 4 star Captain's Club Hotel & Spa is independently owned and prides itself on its attention to detail and personal service.

When you dine at The Club you'll enjoy relaxing in a comfortable contemporary setting while our attentive staff cater to your every need. Customers can gaze out over panoramic views of the picturesque River Stour whilst dining and weather permitting can also dine alfresco on the riverside terrace.

The award winning food is created with passion and expertise using fresh local produce for delicious results. Open to residents and non-residents for breakfast, lunch, afternoon tea or dinner the Captain's Club really is the connoisseurs' choice.

Wick Ferry, Wick Lane, Christchurch, Dorset, BH23 1HU
T: 01202 475111
www.captainsclubhotel.com

Pan fried fillet of Lymington seabass, cauliflower purée, asparagus, warm pea and caper dressing

Serves 4

Ingredients

4 x 200g fillets of seabass

2 x bunches of asparagus

400g fresh podded peas

400g fresh broad beans

Bunch of pea shoots

1 fresh bay leaf

200g butter

100g Lilliput capers

1 lemon

1 head cauliflower

1 litre of semi skimmed milk

4 tablespoons olive oil

Salt and pepper to taste

"This dish is technically simple, but speaks volumes about the produce available on our doorstep here on the South Coast."

Andrew Gault

Method

♦ Chop the head of cauliflower down to small even pieces so it all cooks at the same time. Add to the milk in a saucepan and small pinch of salt and the bay leaf.

♦ Cook on a medium heat until tender, the blend until as smooth as possible, check seasoning and keep warm.

♦ Prepare the asparagus by peeling the outer green skin and chop the dry root end of which can sometimes be quite woody and tough.

- Pod the peas and broad beans and add to a pan of boiling salted water with the asparagus for 1 minute to blanch then refresh in cold water.

- For the fish it's best to use a non-stick pan as the bass skin once descaled is quite nice to eat if crispy. For this, season the fish with salt and pepper and add to the already hot pan skin side down and cook on a medium heat; don't be tempted to move it around, allow it to cook almost completely on the skin side. Once cooked flip it over and the skin should be nice and crisp. Add a knob of cold butter and squeeze of lemon then remove from the pan.

- Keep the cooking juices from the fish to warm the vegetables, that way it keeps all the flavours in the dish, add the asparagus, peas and broad beans, warm through then finally add a little more lemon juice, capers and check the seasoning.

- Dress as per photo and garnish with the pea shoots.

Alan Williams - Highcliff Grill

Alan is currently the Pastry Chef & Junior Sous Chef for the
2 Rosette Highcliff Grill at the Highcliff Marriott in Bournemouth,
working under Matt Budden. Things could have been very different
though; he gave up a decade long career with a High Street Bank to
pursue his dream of becoming a professional chef, beginning less
than four years ago with a first job working for Matt during a stint at
Rhinefield House in the New Forest.

When not at the stove Alan can be found behind the lens of a camera
and some examples of his work can be found in this book as well as
at www.partisanphotography.co.uk

Highcliff Grill

Highcliff Marriott Hotel
St. Michaels Road, West Cliff
Bournemouth, BH2 5DU
T: 01202 200 800

Photo by Alan Williams

Caramelised apple Bakewell tart

"This is the most popular dessert on our menu at the moment and is a version of the classic Bakewell Tart recipe. We serve it with clotted cream, salted caramel, fresh apple and pureed, roasted and chopped almonds." **Alan Williams**

Ingredients

Caramelised apple jam
1.3kg apples; peeled, chopped
1.3kg caster sugar
60g unsalted butter
150ml double cream
1 cinnamon stick
3 cloves
A little water if needed

Cider syrup
200ml dry cider
140g caster sugar
1 cinnamon stick

Frangipane
150g caster sugar
150g unsalted butter
3 eggs
120g ground almonds
15g flour

Sweet pastry
300g flour
150g unsalted butter
60g sugar
3 egg yolks

Photo by Alan Williams

74

Method

- To make the caramelised apple jam, use a large, heavy based saucepan and first heat 300g of the sugar with the butter, mixing the two together until they have reached a nice caramel colour then remove from the heat. Add the cream and whisk together to make a smooth sauce. Mix in everything else and cook out, stirring regularly until it reaches 110°C on a sugar thermometer. This recipe will make far more than you need for this recipe so can be decanted into sterilised jars and used as a regular jam.

- While the jam is cooling, make the sweet pastry. Rub together the flour and butter until roughly breadcrumb like texture. Add the sugar and egg yolks and knead briefly to bring together to a firm dough. Wrap in cling film and chill for an hour.

- To make the frangipane beat the butter and sugar in a mixer until light and fluffy then slowly add the eggs while still mixing, once incorporated fold in the almonds and flour.

- To construct the tart start by rolling out the pastry (take out of the fridge for a little while before to allow it to warm up) and line your tin. Trim off excess and cover with baking paper. Fill the tin with baking beans and blind bake at 160°C for 25 minutes before removing the beans and baking at 180°C for another 12 minutes until golden brown.

- Spread a layer of jam over the pastry and pipe the frangipane on top. Bake at 160°C for approximately 30 minutes until a gentle shake shows that the tart is set.

- While the tart is baking make the cider syrup by combining all of the ingredients and boil together until reduced by one third.

- While the tart is still warm pour the cider syrup over the top and allow it to seep in.

Duet of Spring Dorset Lamb

Recipe on page 34

EXCLUSIVE
BEALES
GOURMET
CATERING

The Bournemouth and Poole College is home to one of the finest catering training establishments in the country, with a national and international reputation for excellence in hospitality and catering training.

The School of Hospitality & Food at the college has recently received recognition from the National Skills Academy (NSA) in hospitality for its Professional Cookery Diploma. The department was awarded a gold award from the newly appointed Hospitality Guild, an AA college rosette for food, was voted Bournemouth's best restaurant in 2011 and is recognised as one of the top twenty catering colleges in the world by the World Association of Chefs.

The College's specialised chefs scholarship programme is arranged by the Royal Academy of Culinary Arts and includes practical training provided by The Ritz, The Dorchester, Claridge's, and the Chewton Glen, to name just a few.

The Bournemouth and Poole College is home to around 11,000 students, offering a broad curriculum in full-time and part-time courses, apprenticeships, foundation degrees and adult learning. The College works closely with the local community and has working relationships with over 2,000 employers, local schools, local government and community groups.

Bournemouth School of Hospitality & Food
The Bournemouth & Poole College

Rising Stars Of The Future

Dusan Osadsky

Adam Baumer

Terry Tomlinson

Thomas Wickens

John Bowler

Dusan Osadsky - Bournemouth & Poole College

Dusan Osadsky is originaly from Slovakia, but moved to Dorset to Study Hospitality and Catering at Bournemouth & Poole College in 2011 to follow his dream and passion to train as a chef.

Dusan started out on a VRQ level 1 course, progressing well and passed with good grades. During the summer of 2012 he was sent away to France on work experience, before returning to study on the VRQ level 2. In September 2013, Dusan will return to the College to study on the VRQ level 3.

Dusan is currently working part time at the Marriott Highcliff Hotel, Bournemouth, as well as attending College.

Fish pie with cider creamed leeks

Serves 4

Ingredients

300g pollock

300g smoked haddock

8 fresh prawns

1 lemon (zest and juice)

1 tsp grain mustard

50g parsley

Pinch of nutmeg

Cider creamed leeks

1 leek

100ml cider

50ml crème fraiche

Velouté

40g butter

40g flour

300ml fish stock

Duchess potato

200g potatoes

2 egg yolks from Blackacre Farm

50g butter

100g cave aged cheddar cheese

Salt and pepper

Method

- Place the fish and prawns in a saucepan, pour in the fish stock and add the parsley stalks and gently simmer until nearly cooked. Carefully remove the fish and prawns from the pan, place neatly in ovenware dishes and set aside. Pass the fish stock through a sieve and keep hot to make the velouté.

- Melt the butter in a thick bottom pan, add the flour, mix well and cook out to a sandy texture over a gentle heat without colouring. Allow the roux to cool slightly.

- Gradually add the hot stock to the roux, stirring or whisking until smooth. Allow to simmer for approximately 10-15 minutes or until the flour has cooked out. Pass through a fine conical strainer.

- Chop the parsley and fold into the velouté along with the grain mustard and squeeze of lemon juice and the zest. Season to taste. Pour the velouté into the dish, coating the fish.

- Peel and cut the potatoes into small even sizes, place in water, bring to the boil and cook until tender.

- When the potatoes are tender, drain off the water and return to the pan, over a low heat to dry out the potato, pass through a medium sieve or mouli.

- Place the potatoes in a clean pan, add the egg yolk, butter and half of the cheese and vigorously stir in with a wooden spoon. Season to taste and place in a piping bag with a star nozzle.

- Pipe the potato neatly on top of the fish mixture, sprinkle a little cheese on top and bake in a hot oven (180°C) for approximately 15-30 minutes.

- Chop the leeks into thin slices, sweat in a pan and add the cider. Reduce the cider by half and fold in the crème fraiche. Serve in a ramekin alongside the fish pie.

- Place the fish pie dish on a plate; serve the leeks in a separate bowl or ramekin.

Adam Baumer – Bournemouth & Poole College

Adam is a 21 year old Apprentice Chef who is currently working at Clayesmore Private School in North Dorset. Adam has recently graduated from his advanced apprenticeship at Bournemouth and Poole College having transferred from Salisbury College after completing his Level 2 Apprenticeship.

Adam is involved in all aspects of kitchen work, including the production and cooking of all meals for the pupils, as well as functions that are hosted at the School. Adam continues also works part time at the Highcliff Marriott Hotel in Bournemouth.

Beef carpaccio, asparagus and parmesan
Serves 2

Ingredients

200g centre-cut beef fillet

3 tbsp olive oil

2 tbsp grain mustard

2 tbsp fennel seeds

2 tbsp coriander seeds

2 tbsp black peppercorns

1 tbsp fresh chopped tarragon

40g parmesan

4 small pluches of salad leaves

12 asparagus spears

Pinch of smoked paprika

40ml oil dressing

Method

- Heat a thin layer of olive oil in a heavy pan; the aim is to sear the beef fillet, not start cooking it, so the pan needs to be really hot. Slowly turn the beef until its coloured all over, including the ends.

- While the fillet is still hot, brush it all over with the grain mustard. Coarsely grind the aromatic fennel seeds, coriander seeds and black peppercorns in a spice or coffee grinder, then spread them out on a plate and roll the fillet in the mix, making sure it's well covered.

- Take a sheet of cling film and roll the beef up as tightly as you can, twisting the ends like a Christmas cracker. Place in the fridge. Ideally you want to leave it overnight for all the flavours to infuse.

- Blanch the asparagus in boiling water for 3 minutes, refresh in ice cold water. Drain and set aside. Peel flakes of parmesan and set aside.

85

- Leave the beef in its cling film. Cut a slice about 1cm thick and remove the cling film. Lay the slice of beef between 2 sheets of plastic (freezer bags are good). Use a meat bat to flatten it; don't bash the life out of it, just bring it down once or twice heavily on the meat. Repeat with the rest of the meat. Place the beef neatly on a plate.

- Arrange the asparagus and parmesan on the plate. Dress the salad leaves and arrange in the middle of the beef.

- Drizzle around the oil dressing and sprinkle a little smoked paprika around the edge.

Terry Tomlinson – Bournemouth & Poole College

Terry is 21 years old and is currently in his final year of an advanced apprenticeship at Bournemouth and Poole College. Terry is currently combining his studies at College whilst working full time as a Chef de Partie at the Custom House Restaurant on Poole Quay.

In 2011 Terry was awarded level 2 *Part Time Student of the Year*, has taken part in the television show 'monster munchies' with the College and went through to the finals of the British Culinary Federations Young Chef of the Year in both 2011 and 2012.

Char grilled chicken Basquaise

Serves 2

Ingredients

1 onion, chopped

1 clove of garlic, finely chopped

½ yellow pepper, thinly sliced

½ red pepper, thinly sliced

1 kg tomatoes, coarsely chopped

6 baby potatoes

2 chicken breasts

Olive oil

100ml red wine sauce

Method

Basquaise garnish

♦   Heat two tablespoons of olive oil in a deep saucepan over medium heat. Add the onions and garlic and cook until golden. Add the peppers and tomato, reduce the heat to low and simmer for about 10-15 minutes stirring every few minutes to prevent it burning. Season with salt and pepper.

Potatoes

♦   Wash and peel the potatoes. Remove both ends to create a nice rounded shape. Blanch in boiling salted water until tender. Drain well.

♦   Heat a frying pan with a little oil, add the potatoes and colour all over, place in an oven to heat through.

Chicken

♦   Brush the chicken breast with a little oil and season with salt and pepper. Place onto a char grill pan skin side down.   **88**

- Sear the chicken until the skin has browned and gone crispy. Transfer onto an oven tray and place in the oven to finish off the cooking process.

- Heat the red wine sauce.

To serve

- Spoon a pile of the Basquaise garnish on to a plate; arrange the potatoes next to it.
- Place the chicken breast whole neatly alongside and drizzle some sauce around the plate.

Thomas Wickens - Bournemouth & Poole College

Thomas Wickens was born in Salisbury, starting his career at the age of 15. Currently working at 1812 in Bournemouth, Thomas has gained experience working at the Old Beams in Ibsley and Chateau De Montreuil in France.

Thomas has just completed a degree at Bournemouth & Poole College and Bournemouth University studying Culinary Arts. After finishing his course in 2013, he now he hopes to expand his culinary experience further by working in France and London.

Thomas has represented the College at competitions, winning medals for his efforts.

Chicken and asparagus mousseline
Serves 2

Ingredients

Mousseline

1 diced chicken breast (skinless)

6 spears of asparagus

1 clove of garlic

10g picked thyme

100ml of double whipped cream

Salt

Asparagus foam

Asparagus peelings

100ml cream

100ml water

Asparagus and scallop tartar

2 scallops

2 spears of asparagus

¼ lemon, juice only

Scallops

4 scallops

10ml oil

10g butter

¼ lemon, juice only

Method

Mousseline

♦ Blend the chicken, garlic, thyme and salt until smooth.
Fold the whipped cream into the mousseline. Peel the asparagus
(save the peelings) and cut in half lengthways. Lay a double
layer of cling film on a worktop then place 6 half asparagus
spears flat side down, pipe the mousseline on top of it in lines.
Roll into a tight cylindrical ballotine. Poach in water slowly
until cooked.

91

- **Asparagus foam:** take any remaining asparagus peelings and blanch in 100ml of cream and100ml water until tender. Remove and blend until a loose puree, to the consistency of single cream, if formed.

- **Asparagus and scallop tartar:** dice two scallops into even sized pieces and finely slice the asparagus. Add a squeeze of lemon juice and season. Chill until ready to serve

- **Scallops:** cut two scallops in half through the middle. Pan fry the scallops in a heavy based pan in oil. Season the scallops and fry on a medium to high heat until golden brown, finish with butter and lemon juice.

- **To serve:** scatter the scallop tartar on the bottom of the plate, slice the mousseline, and place the cooked scallops on the plate, take the loose asparagus foam and aerate with a whisk or hand blender, then place around the plate, finished with mustard cress and lemon oil.

John Bowler - Bournemouth & Poole College

John Bowler was born and raised in the Lake District, Cumbria.
Starting his career as a chef at the age of 16, John studied at a local
catering college before working in many of the area's finest hotels.
At only 19 he became a catering lecturer back at the very college in
which he had trained. Recently John moved to Bournemouth to
continue his education studying a Culinary Arts degree at
Bournemouth and Poole College. He is now studying a Hospitality
Management Degree at Bournemouth University.

Fillet of beef wellington, creamed potato, carrots and spinach

Serves 2

Ingredients

400g beef fillet available from Dorset Charcuteire

2 tbsp olive oil

200g field mushrooms

50g butter

1 large sprig fresh thyme

100ml dry white wine

5 slices prosciutto

250g pack puff pastry

A little flour, for dusting

2 egg yolks beaten with 1tsp water

Garnish

1 kg potatoes, such as Desirée

200g butter, cut into cubes

4 baby carrots

400g spinach

200ml red wine sauce

Method

- Heat an oven to 220°C. Sit the beef fillet on a roasting tray, brush with 1 tbsp olive oil and season with pepper, then roast for 15 minutes for medium-rare or 20 minutes for medium. Remove from the oven and chill in the fridge for 20 minutes.

- While the beef is cooling, coarsely grate the mushrooms. Heat 2 tbsp of the olive oil and 50g butter in a large pan and fry the mushrooms on a medium heat, with 1 large sprig fresh thyme, for about 10 minutes stirring often, until you have a softened mixture.

- Season the mushroom mixture, pour over 100ml white wine and cook for about 10 minutes until all the wine has been absorbed. The mixture should hold its shape when stirred and there should be no liquid. Remove the mushroom duxelle from the pan to cool and discard the thyme.

- Overlap two pieces of cling film over a large chopping board. Lay the slices of prosciutto on the cling film, slightly overlapping, in a double row. Spread half the duxelle over the prosciutto, then sit the fillet on it and spread the remaining duxelle over. Use the cling film's edges to draw the prosciutto around the fillet, then roll it into a sausage shape, twisting the ends of cling film to tighten it as you go. Chill the fillet while you roll out the pastry.

- Dust your work surface with a little flour. Roll out the puff pastry to the thickness of a pound coin laying down, in a rectangle large enough to wrap the beef in. Unravel the fillet from the cling film and sit it length ways to one side of the pastry.

- Beat the 2 egg yolks with 1 tsp water and brush the pastry's edges, then wrap the beef with the remaining pastry. Trim any excess pastry then transfer to a baking tray lined with parchment paper. Glaze all over with more egg yolk and, using the back of a knife, mark the beef Wellington with long diagonal lines, taking care not to cut into the pastry. Chill for at least 30 minutes and up to 24 hours.

- Heat an oven to 200°C. Brush the Wellington with a little more egg yolk and cook until golden, 20-25 minutes for medium-rare beef or 30 minutes for medium. Allow to stand for 10 minutes before serving in thick slices.

Garnish

- For the mash, peel the potatoes and cut into even size dice so they all cook at the same time. Cook for 12-15 minutes in boiling salted water. Drain well and mash the potatoes very thoroughly or press them through a potato ricer or mouli. Gradually beat the butter into the potato until it starts to look shiny, add salt and freshly ground pepper. The potato should become a soft velvety purée. Keep warm until required.

- Boil the carrots in water. Scrape the skin off when cooked. Cut in half, keep warm. Wilt the spinach in a little butter and water. Season to taste. Drain and keep warm.

To serve

- Slice the Wellington into portions. Arrange neatly on the plate and serve with the carrots and spinach and a red wine sauce.

THE
ESCOFFIER
Restaurant

The Escoffier restaurant provides you with a dining experience in a relaxing and unique style, with a menu designed to give you access to an eclectic array of dishes using many local ingredients from local producers.

The Escoffier Restaurant offers a top quality service and opens both at lunch time (with two, three or four course luncheon menus), and three evenings a week serving more formal gourmet and theme menus.

To make a table reservation for the Escoffier Restaurant ring 01202 205874 or e-mail Escoffier@thecollege.co.uk

John Bowler
Photography

Bournemouth & Poole College photographs taken by

John Bowler Photography

98

BLACKACRE FARM
Simply Delicious Free Range Eggs

Founded over 30 years ago by Tim Wood, Blackacre Farm is now run by Tim's son Dan and his wife Briony. Dan, Briony and the family of specially chosen South West farmers that Blackacre works with pour a great deal of time, love and care into their hens, which create what they believe to be the best free-range eggs in the business.

From panoramic Dorset sea views to rolling Somerset fields its girls roam free in some of the most beautiful parts of the country. Each Blackacre Egg is printed with a unique code which will tell you exactly where it has been laid when you enter it on to the website www.blackacrefarmeggs.com and you can find out more about the farmers, their farm and most importantly their chickens!

Blackacre Farm was the first egg producer to win a Gold 1 star in the world-renowned Great Taste Awards. Blackacre Farm Eggs can be found in independent retailers, farm shops, delicatessens and Asda stores throughout the South West and are used by some of the area's most renowned chefs, including Dorset's only Michelin Starred Chef Russell Brown.

 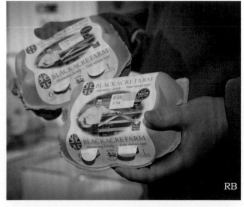

To find out more please visit Blackacre Farm's website or follow the farm on Facebook or twitter @**blackacrefarm**
www,blackacrefarmeggs.com

Introducing

Chef Gary Kilminster

Chef Alistair John Willies

Chef Ryan Hopper MCCGC

Chef Chris Weight

Chef Loic Gratadoux

Gary Kilminster – Bournemouth & Poole College

Trained at the Bournemouth & Poole College from 1997-2000, Gary has a wealth of experience as a chef, including positions working at The De Vere Royal Bath Hotel, The House of Commons, The De Vere Belfry, Whittlebury Hall, Management Training Centre Hotel & Spa, Suvretta House Hotel, Careys Manor Hotel and as a personal chef aboard a luxury charter yacht, Masquerade of Sole, in the Mediterranean. Since 1997 Gary has competed in over 50 competitions here and abroad, winning 35 medals and trophies including: The William Heptinstall Scholarship 2002, First in Class and best of the day Food Hygiene Live Theatre Hotelympia 2002, The Midlands Association of Chefs Young Chef of the Year 2003 and the 2005 Dorset & Hampshire Chef of the Year. In 2013 her was awarded the Ken Fraser MBE Memorial Award for Education by the British Culinary Federation. Gary is involved in this project in memory of his Grandad, Frank Blades, who passed away in Forest Holme in 2008.

Photograph by Alan Williams

Smoked chicken and ham carbonara
Serves 2

Ingredients

200g fresh egg tagliatelle

50g smoked chicken

1 shallot

50g mushrooms

50g cooked ham

50ml white wine

50ml Chicken stock

100g cream cheese

10g flat leaf parsley, chopped

30g parmesan cheese

(half grated, half flaked)

10ml oil

Method

♦   Peel and dice the shallot, set aside. Cut the mushrooms into quarters, set aside.

♦   Cut the chicken and ham into bite size pieces, set aside.

♦   In a deep pan fry the shallot in a little oil until soft, place in the mushrooms and fry for 2-3 minutes. Add the white wine and reduce by half. Add the chicken stock and bring to the boil. Fold in the chicken and ham and allow to heat through.

♦   Fold in the cream cheese and the grated parmesan.

♦   Bring to the boil a saucepan of water, when boiling, add 1 tbsp of oil. Add the tagliatelle and allow to cook for 3-4 minutes.

♦   Drain the tagliatelle through a colander. Return to the pan.

♦   Spoon the carbonara over the tagliatelle and mix well. Divide two portions into serving bowls and sprinkle on the flaked parmesan and parsley.

Alistair John Willies - New Westcliff Hotel

Alistair was initially trained at Barnfield College in Luton, Bedfordshire. After this he worked in several catering establishments training as a pastry Chef. During the 90's Alistair moved down to London where he took a position at The Park Lane Hotel in Picadilly. Following this he moved on to the world famous Harrods department store in Knightsbridge gaining further experience as a Pastry Chef. During Alistair's time at Harrods a position came up at a brand new restaurant called Launceston Plaice in the Kensington Muses, run by the celebrity Chef Rolly Lee. Following several years working in and around London, Alistair decided to take another huge challenge by moving to Guernsey where he gained a Salon Culinaire Third Place for Pastry, resulting in him being head-hunted and consequently working in several private hotels for a period of five years. In 1995 Alistair moved back to England, where he found work in The New Forest and Bournemouth area. In 2011 Alistair joined the New Westcliff Hotel, under the ownership of Mr Paul Hedges. Together they are endeavouring to bring a new style of cuisine made up of good quality local produce which is presented in a modern style. **106**

New Westcliff Hotel

The New Westcliff Hotel is set conveniently on the prestigious West Cliff side of Bournemouth which gives easy access to the beach and the town centre and shops. The hotel itself was originally two Victorian buildings that have been connected to make the hotel as it is. The hotel offers complimentary facilities such as; an indoor leisure suite with heated swimming pool, sauna and jacuzzi, private cinema and bowls rink with use of woods.

Alistair prides himself on producing a fresh daily menu that incorporates from fresh local produce with a high standard of presentation. The hotel can cater for people with most dietary needs with a little notice, ensuring that we have something to tempt everyone's taste buds.

The New Westcliff Hotel prides itself on a warm friendly service that keeps guests returning to them time and again.

27-29 Chine Crescent, West Cliff, Bournemouth, Dorset, BH2 5LB

T: 01202 551062

www.newwestcliffhotel.co.uk

Confit of duck leg in an orange, sultana and chilli sauce

Serves 4

Ingredients

4 duck legs

1 onion, finely chopped

1 leek, finely chopped

1 carrot, finely chopped

1 red chilli, finely chopped

4 juniper berries

1000ml orange juice

25g sultanas

Method

♦ In a pan, lightly sauté the onion, leek, carrot and half of the chilli. Set aside in an oven tray.

♦ Trim the duck legs, removing the knuckle and any excess fat.

♦ Place the duck legs on the vegetables and cover with the orange juice, make sure the legs are fully covered.

♦ Cover with a lid or tin foil and place in a pre-heated oven at approximately 120°C for three hours.

♦ After three hours remove the tray from the oven and take the duck legs out of the cooking liquid.

♦ Pass the cooking liquid through a fine sieve and leave to stand for 10-15 minutes. This allows the impurities to rise to the top.

♦ Using a ladle, skim the fat to leave a clean liquid.

♦ Place the liquid into a saucepan and place on a low heat to reduce the cooking liquid by half. Prior to serving add the sultanas and the rest of the chilli to the sauce

♦ To reheat the duck for serving, place the duck legs on a tray into a hot oven (180°C) for 8-10 minutes.

♦ When ready, serve the duck on a plate dressed in the sauce. **108**

Ryan Hopper MCCGC

Ryan Hopper MCCGC left the Royal Navy in April 2010 after serving for 23½ years. During his time he cooked for many VIPs including HRH The Queen, The Prince and Princess of Wales and many other members of our and foreign royal families. During his time in the Royal Navy Ryan was the Senior Military Craft Instructor at HMS Raleigh, training naval chef recruits to NVQ Level 2. He was also the captain of the Naval Service Culinary Arts Team and also the Combined Services Culinary Arts Team, where he achieved double gold medals at the 2006 and 2010 Culinary World Cup and gold and silver at the 2008 Culinary Olympics.

Ryan holds the position of team captain for the Craft Guild of Chefs Culinary Academy Team and is also a Master Craftsman, Craft Guild of Chefs. Ryan is based in Poole and is currently working as the Group Executive Chef for Defence, Compass Group ESS, overseeing 34 kitchens across the South Coast.

Pan seared halibut,
cream poached sweet potato pearls, heart of palm
Serves 4

Ingredients

500g halibut fillet

150g butter

100ml olive oil

500g sweet potato

100ml vegetable stock

200ml double cream

400g hearts of palm

Seasoning to taste

Micro herbs to garnish

Method

♦   Peel the sweet potato and with melon baller, scoop out one inch
    (2.5cm) pearls. Cut the pearls in half. Pour the cream and
    vegetable stock into a pot and bring to a simmer. Add the sweet
    potato to the pot. When tender remove sweet potato and reduce
    the cream to a coating consistency.

♦   Trim and cut halibut into four even size pieces, lightly dusting
    the skin side. Heat the frying pan, add butter and oil. Place fish
    to the pan, skin side down, and cook until golden and the skin
    has crisped. Turn fish and remove pan from heat.

♦   Remove fish from pan to draining cloth. Return pan to heat and
    then pan fry heart of palms until golden. Remove and drain.
    Cut lengthways and then in half. Dress onto plate.
    Add sweet potato back to reduction, warm, then dress over
    hearts of palm. Place halibut on top. Garnish with herbs.

Chris Weight - Cobham Sports and Social Club

Chris began his cooking career under the direction of Bernard Blake at the Royal George Hotel at the young age of fourteen. He then went on to study at the RTC Galway for two years whilst working at the Great Southern Hotel. Chris's next career move led him to Killarney where he worked at the Lake Hotel before moving to England.

Chris worked in London establishments for two years before moving to the south of England and working in hotels and restaurants locally. In the early nineties Chris moved into pub management with Morlands Brewery of Abingdon but continued to work in the kitchens whilst his wife looked after front of house.

In 1998 he took over the running of Cobhams Sports Club at Merley and is still there to this day. Chris continues to run a very busy establishment with a great reputation for food. **112**

Cobham Sports and Social Club

Cobham Sports and Social Club was set up in 1971 by Sir Alan Cobham for his staff and their families. It was later opened up to friends of family and it now has a membership of over 2,000 people.

With conference rooms that can hold parties from 20 to 200 it is in constant use for anniversaries, weddings, private parties, birthdays, local societies, conferences and a Sunday Carvery that serves fresh home cooked food.

The kitchen provides a wide array of dishes for buffets and set dinners to a la Carte Menus in the members lounge.

The Club also has a great nine hole golf course, large modern children's play area football pitch, squash courts, model steam railway, petanque courts, jive and line dance classes, fly fishing section, bridge club, country music club, wine tasters and many other sections.

"Probably one of the most successful clubs in the south of England"
Chris Weight

Tel: 01202 885773

Photos by Richard Budd

Smoked haddock Florentine
Serves 4

Ingredients

Mashed potato
1kg Desiree potatoes

50g butter

Salt and pepper

Warm milk

Smoked haddock
4 x 140g boneless, smoked haddock fillets

500ml semi skimmed milk

6 black peppercorns

Small onion

Bayleaf

Cheese sauce
115g Cheddar cheese

50g butter

50g plain white flour

500ml milk

1 tsp English mustard

Spinach
A large bag of baby spinach leaves

25g butter

Salt and pepper

Poached eggs
4 free range eggs

Photo by Richard Budd

Method

- **Making the mashed potato:** Peel and cut potatoes into evenly sized cubes. Bring salted water to the boil and cook for 25 minutes. Drain and return over heat to remove excess water. Put potatoes through a ricer to remove any lumps, then add the butter. Add a little warm milk to the potatoes until light and fluffy. Season and reserve for later.

- **Cooking the haddock:** Bring the milk to the boil with a bayleaf, 6 peppercorns and thinly sliced onion. Add the haddock fillets and cook gently for approximately 4 minutes. Remove the haddock and keep warm.

- **Making the cheese sauce:** Melt the butter in a pan and add the flour. Slowly add the milk to the flour and butter mix, stirring continuously. Add the grated cheese, mustard and pepper.

- **Cooking the spinach:** Melt the butter, add the spinach, cook until softened and season.

- **Cooking the poached eggs:** Bring water to the boil in a wide rimmed casserole type pan and then turn down the temperature so that the water is gently boiling. Crack each of the eggs in a cup and then gently tip the egg into the water one at a time. Cook for three minutes and then remove using a slotted spoon.

- **To assemble**: Reheat your mash potato gently in a pan and place in the centre of a plate or pasta bowl. Top with some spinach and place a haddock fillet on the spinach. Top with a poached egg and coat with the cheese sauce.

Loic Gratadoux - Head Chef, Harbour Heights Hotel

French-born Loic has been back to the FJB Collection having previously worked at the Sandbanks based Harbour Heights Hotel as junior sous chef between 2007 and 2008.

Born in France, Loic was introduced to good food and fine wines from a young age. With a strong family and cultural heritage, coming from the South West Coast where the seafood is king, it quickly became a strong passion of his. He has always believed that classical combinations of flavours are made to be played with and brought up to date with a modern twist.

He studied at the Ecole Superieure de Cuisine Française before spending two years at La Table du Lancaster in Paris working with master chef Michel Troisgros. He has also had numerous work experiences in Michelin starred restaurants in France (Le Relais de la Poste, The Eiffel Tower, and l'Arpege). Following a move to England, he became head chef at Christchurch Harbour Hotel where he worked for four years before taking on the head chef position at the Harbour Heights last year. Since then the Harbar restaurant has been a valuable tool for expressing his passion of food.

HARBOUR HEIGHTS

The boutique Harbour Heights Hotel in Sandbanks, Poole, is quite simply, contemporary elegance at its very best.
The breathtaking views are unique, changing continually with the seasons. Serving exquisite, award-winning cuisine complemented by an extensive cellar of fine wines, Harbour Heights Hotel makes any visit special.
The floor-to-ceiling glass windows mean that you can enjoy the glorious views whatever the weather.
The south-facing teak-decked terrace makes the most of the sun at any time of day. So you may enjoy a leisurely alfresco meal or simply drink in the views.
Savour the delights of their two AA Rosettes restaurant and enjoy a warm welcome on every visit.

Harbour Heights Hotel, 73 Haven Road, Sandbanks, Poole, Dorset
www.harbourheights.com

Tiger prawn and cuttlefish
Serves 4

Ingredients

4 large tiger prawns, shells on

1 cuttlefish medium size (ask the fishmonger to clean it for you)

1 red pepper

1 yellow pepper

1 red onion

1 red chilli

1 bunch of coriander

2 lemons

Extra virgin olive oil

Sherry vinegar

Salt

Pepper

Sugar

Smoked paprika

Method

- Separate the tentacles from the body of the cuttlefish.
  Cook the body in four pieces and score with a sharp knife to
  allow an even cooking. Cook in boiling water for only a minute
  (more than this and they will become tough). Allow the cuttlefish
  to cool down and cut the tentacles from the base.

- Then, get the marinade ready for the tentacles. Finely dice the
  peppers, red onion, chili and coriander, mix together with
  100ml of extra virgin olive oil, 20ml of sherry vinegar and the
  juice of a lemon. Adjust the seasoning with salt, pepper, a touch
  of sugar and smoked paprika.

- Add the tentacles and allow to marinate in the fridge for at least
  2 hours before serving.

- Peel the tiger prawns, leaving the head and the tail on (it gives
  more flavour), and keep in the fridge until ready to use.

- To finish the dish, start by pan frying the tiger prawn for
  1-2 minutes on each side. When the prawn is nearly ready,
  pan fry the cuttlefish (this must be very quick otherwise the
  cuttlefish will become tough).

- To assemble; start by putting the marinated tentacles in the
  centre of the plate, this will be the base of your dish, then add
  the cuttlefish and the tiger prawn. Add a gentle squeeze of
  lemon and it's ready to eat.

Essential Cuisine

Essential Cuisine cooking stocks are made with the serious home chef in mind.

We recognise a need for a high quality stock that helps the nations home chefs get the very best from their stews, casseroles, braises, pies, soups, risottos, gravies and sauces. Made to taste just like your own kitchen-made stock, with the appropriate level of salt and fat, each 96g pot makes up to 8 litres of gorgeous, tasty stock giving your dish the balance and depth of flavour that is hard to find amongst other manufactured stocks. With a range of stocks that includes chicken, beef, vegetable, fish, veal and lamb, they are perfect to use when making restaurant-quality and professional standard dishes.

Rated by Good Food Magazine as the best powdered stocks in the country, each pot of stock is that essential pantry ingredient perfect for time poor home chefs who simply don't have time to make a kitchen made stock. Convenient, easy to use and with a long shelf life – taste the difference today. Sold in more than 200 farm shops, delis, high quality butchers as well as available in Harvey Nichols, Divertimenti, Partridges and at

www.essentialcuisine.com/homechef

Maciek Kijewski
Beales Gourmet Ltd

Introducing

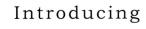

Celebrity Chef Lesley Waters

Celebrity Chef Ashley Palmer-Watts

Lesley Waters - Lesley Waters Kitchen

Well known for her regular television appearances on Ready Steady
Cook, Great Food Live and This Morning, Lesley is also a former
Head Tutor of Leith's School of Food & Wine, author of several
Cookery Books, a qualified Fitness Instructor and a mother of two!
Originally a Londoner born and bred, Lesley was quickly charmed by
the beauty of the West Dorset area and inspired by the superb quality
of the fresh local produce available right on her doorstep. She likes to
cook seasonal food whenever possible and her simple, modern style
creates dishes that are easy to recreate with stunning results.
Teaching has always been her great passion and opening her own
Cookery School in this amazing location is the realisation of a long
held dream. Her energetic style of presentation is expertly combined
with clear and simple guidance, making her classes both entertaining
and informative. Lesley has recently been filming a new series with
BBC1 'Put your menu where your mouth is' and has recently opened
her first restaurant, Lesley Waters Kitchen, in the West Country.

Lesley Waters Cookery School

Lesley Waters Cookery School at Abbot's Hill Farm nestles in the heart of the West Dorset countryside. It is about fresh, simple ingredients and creating great food. But it's not just about the cooking - it's the whole day, meeting people and enjoying the atmosphere where you can relax, learn and laugh. We pride ourselves on creating a relaxed and friendly atmosphere and you will take home with you the knowledge and the know how to create simple and stylish food with confidence and flair. No expert skills are needed, you just need to enjoy food and good company. The school offers a wide range of interesting one and two day hands on and demonstration days for all abilities, including Bread and Baking, Cooler than Chillies, By the Sea, Seasonal Kitchen and the all new Shine course.

Please see www.lesleywaters.com to find out what Lesley has been up to and for more details of the courses.

E: info@lesleywaters.com **T**: 0844 800 4633

Roasted salmon with broad bean salsa verde

Serves 4

Ingredients

For the salmon

3 courgettes, grated

1 lemon, zest only

60ml olive oil

2 tail end pieces salmon fillet

(900g each, pin boned with skin on)

For the Salsa Verde

100g baby broad beans

(cooked and podded)

4 tbps flat leaf parsley

2 tbsp fresh mint leaves

2 garlic cloves, crushed

99g jar capers, drained and rinsed

150ml olive oil

Method

♦   Pre-heat the oven to 200°C.

♦   Grate the courgettes and place in a bowl with the lemon zest, 30ml olive oil and season generously.

♦   Put one salmon fillet, skin side down, on a roasting tray. Spread over the courgette mixture then put the other fillet on top skin side up. Tie up with string every 2.5cm. Drizzle over remaining oil and season with a little sea salt. Roast for 35-40 minutes or until just cooked through.

♦   Meanwhile, make the salsa verde. Put the broad beans, parsley, mint, garlic, capers and oil into a food processor. Whizz for just a few seconds until it has a coarse texture. Season to taste.

♦   Remove the salmon from the oven and place onto a serving dish. Serve with the salsa verde and roasted new potatoes.

Ashley Palmer-Watts – Executive Head Chef, Fat Duck Group

Originally from Dorset, Ashley Palmer-Watts's love of food began with his love of the countryside and his familiarity with the seasons and exceptional produce of the British Isles. An after-school washing up job in a local restaurant at thirteen ignited a passion for cooking that has resulted in a career spanning almost twenty years. After leaving school, he started to work at Le Petit Canard in Dorset where he learnt the fundamental disciplines of the kitchen whilst spending most of his free time visiting producers and suppliers.

Ashley joined Heston Blumenthal at The Fat Duck in Bray in 1999 when it had just received its first star. Within two years, he was promoted to Sous Chef and he became Head Chef in 2003. Since 2008, he has been the Executive Head Chef for the Fat Duck group. Ashley currently heads up the kitchen at *Dinner by Heston Blumenthal* at the Mandarin Oriental, Hyde Park.

His creative eye for detail coupled with a great enthusiasm for research and British ingredients have enabled him to create the unique menu of historically inspired British dishes with Heston Blumenthal for the new restaurant. He continues to oversee development at The Fat Duck and The Hinds Head and The Crown Pub in Bray.

Roast scallop, samphire, pickled dulse and clam broth
Serves 2

Ingredients & Method

Pickled Dulse

360g water

72g chardonnay vinegar

5g sugar

4g salt

35g white soy sauce

20g dried dulse

♦ In a pan, heat the water, chardonnay vinegar and white soy.

♦ Add the sugar and salt, stir until dissolved.

♦ Remove from the heat and leave to fully cool.

♦ Thoroughly wash the dried dulse in cold running water to remove any sand. Leave to soak for 10 minutes.

♦ Strain the dulse, leave to drain.

♦ Add the re-hydrated dulse to the cooled pickling liquid.

♦ Place the pickled dulse into the fridge to pickle for 24 hours.

Vegetable stock

250g leeks, white part only, sliced

200g carrots, grated

175g onions, sliced

175g button mushrooms, grated

85g fennel, grated

85g celery, sliced

40g olive oil

1 bay leaf

4 thyme sprigs

1.5 litres cold water

25g flat leaf parsley

- In a large pan add the olive oil and the grated, sliced vegetables and sweat without colour for 5 minutes.
- Add the bay and thyme. Add the water, bring to the boil.
- Skim off any scum or impurities that rise to the surface. Gently simmer for 30 minutes.
- Remove from the heat, add the parsley and allow to infuse for 20 minutes.
- Pass the stock through a fine sieve and discard the vegetables.
- Remove any fat from the surface of the stock and refrigerate until required.

Scallops

6 scallops

250g clams

5g chopped garlic

20g samphire

10g rock samphire

30g bulb spring onions

(sliced finely and soaked in water)

20g pickled dulse

(plus a couple pieces for finishing)

5g chopped coriander

80g vegetable stock

15g pickle liquid from the dulse

Squeeze of lemon

- Roast the scallops in a pan until light golden. Remove and set aside in a warm place to rest and complete cooking.
- Heat a small amount of olive oil in a frying pan, add the washed clams and cook on high heat for 1 minute.
- Add the chopped garlic and cook for a further minute. Add the vegetable stock, both samphire's and place a lid on top, cook for a further minute to open the clams.

- Add the chopped coriander, sliced onions, pickle liquid and a squeeze of lemon juice.
- Place a small spoon of the broth mix into the centre of the bowl, arrange the 3 scallops and spoon the remaining clams and samphire around.
- Place a couple of larger pieces of pickled dulse in and around and serve.

BLACKACRE FARM
Simply Delicious Free Range Eggs

Photo by Richard Budd

The Lyme Bay Winery, originally Lyme Bay Cider Co., was founded on a dream to leave the City and return to the West Country to live. With a passion to make a real West Country cider, and inspired by the local Lyme Bay coastline, at first they produced just draught and bottled ciders, supplying local pubs and shops.

Over time Lyme Bay Cider Co. began making other traditional drinks, rediscovering the tipples country folk have always made and bringing them back to life. Many of these traditional country wines and fruit liqueurs have developed a real following and now they make a large range of award-winning drinks.

All of the drinks are hand-made, by a small team of individuals, who utilise both traditional and modern production techniques to create the best quality tipples they can.

In 2012 at The Great Taste Awards, Lyme Bay Winery received a Triple-Gold Star for Jack Ratt Vintage Dry Cider, a Two-Star Gold for Jack Ratt Scrumpy Cider, Two-Star Gold for Ginger Wine and One-Star Gold for Christmas Mead.

www.lymebaywinery.co.uk

Dorset On A Plate - The Story

In August 2012, I was approached by Gary Kilminster from Bournemouth and Poole College who was interested in fundraising for Forest Holme Hospice Charity. Gary had a personal experience with Forest Holme Hospice after his Grandad received care during his battle against a life limiting illness. After our initial meeting Gary and I realised that we shared a common interest in food, chefs and local restaurants. We decided to use our passion for local produce to collaborate on a cook book that would showcase the best of what Dorset has to offer. This led to the development of our idea for 'Dorset On A Plate'.

In order to raise the funds to cover the print costs of the book, we hosted an evening of culinary delights at the Marriott Hotel in Bournemouth. Four of Dorset's top chefs treated diners to a unique four course meal that showcased local produce and suppliers (Pictured right). The remainder of funding for the book was kindly donated by our book sponsors; Beales Gourmet Ltd, Blackacre Farm and Ashley Press Printers.

Gary and I would like to take this opportunity to thank all of the chefs that have contributed to this book. We would like to say a special thank you to Russell Brown, Richard Allsopp and Matt Budden for helping us to raise the funds to have the book printed.

We hope that you enjoy reading our book and take the time to visit some of Dorset's finest restaurants. Profits from the sale of this book will go towards end-of-life care at Forest Holme Hospice.

ASHLEY PRESS

EST. 1932

Family Run Business
Since 1932

Digital and Litho Printers
Mono to Full Colour Print
Design or Direct from File to Print

stationery • business cards
leaflets • brochures • booklets
personalised print • labels
posters • canvas prints • artwork

Tel: 01202 737744 **Email:** sales@ashleypress.co.uk

www.ashleypress.co.uk

Unit 2 Brixey Business Park
18-26 Fancy Road
Poole   Dorset   BH12 4PZ

Richard Budd - Photographer

Richard Budd is a creative and versatile photographer and designer. He works in all areas of photography from food to theatre, and including weddings and live events. He is an expert in lighting and shooting "in camera" so you can see the results as you work with him. Richard is based in Dorset and travels throughout the UK and abroad. He is also the co-founder of the Key to the Future Charity, working to help people deprived of education because of civil war in Sudan.

"Wherever I am and whatever the subject I thoroughly enjoy the challenge of creating something remarkable and new. My design background is invaluable when it comes to creating images for magazines and books and it enables me to work closely with editors to achieve their aims as well as my own. I love the variety of photography, one day I'll be photographing goats, the next I'll be at the top of a sculpture made from shipping containers photographing crazy French artists!"

Examples of Richard's work can be viewed at

www.RichardBudd.co.uk

T: 07767-895205

E: Richard@RichardBudd.co.uk

Index

Chefs

Adam Baumer	84
Alan Williams	72
Alistair John Willies	106
Andrew Gault	68
Ashley Palmer-Watts	130
Chris Weight	112
Colin Nash	52
Dusan Osadsky	80
Gary Kilminster	102
Ian Gibbs	44
Jack Ingram	62
John Bowler	93
Lesley Waters	126
Loic Gratadoux	116
Luke Stuart	40
Maciek Kijewski	32
Matt Budden	18
Richard Allsopp	22
Russell Brown	12
Ryan Hopper	110
Simon Hallam	48
Terry Tomlinson	87
Thomas Wickens	90